A Revelation
Walking Backwards
Into The Footsteps
Of Saint Solange

Dr. Solanges Vivens

A Revelation

Images of Saint Solange Church and Saint Solange Chapel by Clifford Barnes Esq. and Dr. Solanges Vivens

International Standard Book Number 978-0-9970413-2-3
Library of Congress Control Number 2016939137

Published in the United States of America

A Revelation

The author proceeds from this book will go to the

renovation project of the Saint Solange Chapel.

For additional information, please visit

www.arevelationgetthebook.com

FORWARD

All of our lives are lived with a special spiritual connection to God. This book is a story about that special spiritual connection. It's about two kindred spirits with the same name, Solange. Both grew up in a world that harbored dangers at every turn and both would use that danger to manifest their faith and glorify God.

A sweet adolescent girl named Solange born in another time and another place would give her life to Christ at a very young age. Her namesake Solanges, born centuries later with the same fervor to do God's bidding. Trust in the Lord for he has promised his comfort no matter what we face in this lifetime, no matter what calamity comes our way, great or small, God will never leave us. He will be there in good times and in bad times, pouring

out his love, giving us wisdom and guiding us to safety.

This is an amazing story of how we love and how the spirit of sisterhood connects lives lived centuries apart.

The journey begins when God places a simple question in the heart of one Solanges in the year 2015. This question unites her with her soul sister Solange who lived in the 9th century. It is a story of how the challenges both women face in their lifetimes lead to the joy, comfort and peace they both share with the world.

Be strong and do not give up, for your work will be rewarded with Gods' blessing.

~Your Goddaughter: Ingrid Mitchell

A REVELATION

Special thanks to Mrs. Jocelyn Francmont whom I met at the Church of Saint Solange on my first day in Bourges, France. Thank you for taking the time to show me around and educate me about Saint Solange.

Thanks to Josiane and Jacques Tixier for providing me with love and room & board for the three weeks while I waited for Pentecostal Monday.

Come with me on an incredible spiritual journey. It will take you across continents, centuries and cultures. This through the spirit of a Haitian born business woman who becomes spiritually connected to a 9th century martyred saint from France in such an amazing way, I know our paths could not have crossed by accident.

It was indeed a divine appointment that has developed into a sacred mission. How else can I explain how I found her? Or did she find me? How else do you explain what caused me to leave my comfortable home in Washington DC to spend thousands of dollars and hundreds of hours researching the internet and traveling impulsively to France to satisfy a curiosity?

This was a calling that I would not fully understand until the questions in my own heart could be answered. When this journey began, I did

suspect in the deepest sense that in some ethereal way my purpose was and is somehow intertwined with Saint Solange.

Now however, after much travel and research I know without a doubt, that the revelation of Saint Solange and finding out who she was, is my divine assignment. Introducing her to millions of people today and understanding how her life has paralleled and impacted my life and the life of others is now a life calling for me.

I can now empathize with the great patriarch Abraham who was called out of his country Ur to go somewhere that had no meaning to him until he arrived where God told him to go. Could that be my route as well? In a real sense I did not know where this deep yearning was leading, but not to start on the quest I felt would leave me as emotionally

barren as a mother whose womb could not bring forth new life. With that deep sense of responsibility and mission I cannot rest until this sacred mission is accomplished.

As expected, because of the time in which Saint Solange was born and lived, biographical information about her is questionable. As I searched through scores of historical records to put together enough facts to bring to life this mysterious person, my yearning for more drastically increased with each discovery I made.

I found out that Solange was born in the year 863, in Villemont, a small town in the province of Berry in Bourges, France.

Villemont is about a mile from the parish of Saint Martin du Crot, a church that today still honors Saint Solange as its namesake. Solange was born to poor parents who lived a devout Christian

lifestyle. Religion played a very large role in lives of children at that time. Children were educated in schools, churches or at home. At an early age, stories of holy personages such as St. Denis the patron saint of Paris, who suffered persecution to establish a base in Gaul (now France) was a logical curriculum choice.

At the same time there was an ever increasing veneration of the Virgin Mary and Mary Magdalene as evidence of an elevated standing of female Christians. The Virgin Mary, the mother of Jesus carried the title of Mother of God and Queen of Heaven. As a result of this exulted status, in the year 863 the "Feast of Our Lady" was declared. This holy day was declared of equal importance to those of Easter and Christmas.

The feast of Mary Magdalene, who was to witness the post resurrection of Jesus, was also celebrated in earnest as well.

With such emphasis on Christian education, vocations such as nuns for girls and monks for boys were encouraged and celebrated. Solange herself made a vow of chastity at the age of seven. At that time it was not unusual for children to talk of marriage at such a young age. Her choice of chastity however meant she would live her life married to Jesus. This declaration and dedication placed her in position to pursue her vocation as a nun.

As she grew, stories of miracles and other apparitions developed around her. Legend holds that one day while Solange, a shepherdess was tending sheep in her father's field near her home, she was observed to be praying.

A bright star of heavenly brilliance shone over her head. This was a sign of her closeness to God. Solange was also reported to have the gift of healing not only for her fellow neighbors but animals as well. Healing the sick, blind and deaf, along with providing relief from natural disasters were some of the miraculous events attributed to Saint Solange. Even after her death many other miracles were accredited to Saint Solange.

Young and very attractive, there were no doubts that there were admirers who were attracted not only to her spiritual qualities but also her beauty. One such admirer was Bernard, a son of the Count of Poitiers, who became mesmerized by the teenage shepherdess he saw tending her father's flock. As the story goes, he made advances toward her that were refused on the grounds that

she was married to Christ. Her resistance infuriated Bernard. Perhaps he thought it was beneath him or maybe it was simply the arrogance of a wealthy nobleman, rebuffed and angered by the rejection of a lowly shepherd girl. Bernard found that he was no longer able to control his impulses, so one evening, he seized the opportunity to kidnap Solange while she was alone tending to the sheep. Bernard dragged her onto his horse and carried her away. Much to his surprise, Solange put up such a gallant fight that as they were crossing the river, they both fell in. Bernard, an experienced horseman became so enraged that he chased after Solange on foot. As he charged after her with his sword drawn out and extended, with a swift slicing motion, he decapitated Solange.

The beheading of Saint Solange

Legend says that as her head was falling, this Virgin of Villemont caught it with her hands, and recited the name of Jesus three times and walked with her detached head in her hands, nearly a mile to the church of Saint Martin, where she later died and was buried.

Saint Solange carrying her head

None of this did I know about Saint Solange. In fact it was not until mid-March 2015, that I even heard of a Solange who is a saint. It all started at about 3 am. A sleepless night turned into a restless early morning as I tossed and turned. Finally, I found it was best to rise from my bed in my Florida home where I was spending a couple of the winter months away from Washington DC.

My bedroom is on the lake side of the house. At that time there were no curtains over the sliding glass doors, so the open area allowed my eyes to continue roaming towards the lake. It was a clear night and the moon created a shadow of the trees reflected in the lake. Not wanting to disturb the others in the household, I decided to grab my cell phone and for some unexplained reason, googled "Angel of the Sun" which is the meaning of the

word Solange. "Angel of the Sun" is the title of the book I am now currently writing.

Using my life experiences as my subject, the book describes the life of a girl born in Port-au-Prince, Haiti to very poor parents who immigrated to the United States of America and became a successful entrepreneur.

After I completed some initial research, my mind wandered and I remembered that before I left for Florida, my Executive Administrative Assistant was listening to an audio book, while working on the computer. Since I was only one door away, I could not help but hear that one of the girls in the audio book was named Solange. I became curious about her book since I was also in the process of writing my own. As a result the origin of the name Solange became a question in my mind.

Being awake and restless I decided it was a great time to research the name Solange while researching the title of my book "Angel of the Sun".

In this modern day and time we no longer have to make a trip to the library to do research. Google makes a vast amount of information so readily available that we can research anything at any time, even while in bed in our pajamas. I googled the word Solange and to my surprise I came across the picture of a beheaded body of a woman named Saint Solange.

Statue of the beheaded Saint

"What is this?" I asked in amazement. How could I have arrived into my late sixties and was never aware that there was a saint by the name Solange? I continue to read. As a result, the more I read, the more a feeling of similarities came upon me. It was no longer just her name. Her life, even as distant in time and place from mine, resounded with a feeling of connectedness and yes, even a feeling of familiarity.

As I continued to read about Saint Solange, the similarities became more and more astonishing. Here I am born in Port-au-Prince, Haiti, from poor parents just like Saint Solange. My mother never finished school, never worked outside of her home and spent her life caring for her house and her children. My father, similarly educated as my mother was a hardworking man and the only

breadwinner. My parents lived and taught us a devout Christian lifestyle similar to Saint Solange's parents. Of course neither of my parents, both born in Haiti, knew anything about a French saint named Solange, nor a place called Bourges in France. They were oblivious to all these details yet for some still unexplained reason, they named me, their fifth child, Solange.

Why Solange? For 68 years I had never raised this question. But today, the question reminds me of a dream I had as a teenager where I stood at the top of a staircase leading down to a dimly lit basement. I stood there wondering what would happen if I descended. Would there be something spooky down there or a dazzling treasure? Would there be a gift just for me? Standing there I felt both fright and great expectation. If I kept going

down there, something terrible could be hiding there, but if I turned around and went back up, I'd spend hours maybe years wondering what great thing I had missed. I awoke without knowing what choice I made. Down or up. I always believed I fought my fears and descended because I felt joy and happiness when I awoke. I had not discovered some great gift but felt I had overcome the fears and rigors of stepping into the unknown and come through successfully. That barrier had been broken.

In somewhat the same way, I knew eventually I would have to confront this current mystery. I needed to charge ahead or forever wonder what would have happened if only I had followed my heart.

Adding to the intrigue, was each time I unearthed a new detail aligning me with Saint

Solange like spiritually conjoined twins, another revelation would surface that would pull me deeper into the mystery. Sometimes I felt like detective Peter Falk in the TV show Columbo who was always chasing that "just one more thing."

The greatest mind-blowing discovery that unquestionably sealed Saint Solange and I together came from a Google search that revealed the feast day of Saint Solange is celebrated annually on May 10th. "This can't be," I said to myself. I was born on May 10th. So is anyone to believe that my parents, who knew nothing about this Saint could arrange it so that I was born on the very same day that Saint Solange died? That is so impossible that one must move from the realm of the physical to the supernatural. Only God could orchestrate something like this. Isn't this what life's greatest mysteries are all about? Are such mysteries too complex for the human mind to grasp or to fathom without spiritual understanding?

Those startling facts made me sit straight up in my bed. I cautioned myself to pay attention to what I was reading. I could feel goose pimples starting to emerge on my arms. "Is this for real?" "Where is this coming from?" I asked myself again and again. My curiosity grew so much that I put down my cell phone and picked up my laptop to better research all the questions that were pouring from my pores.

In a worldwind of non-stop research, the similarities between the Saint and me continued revealing themselves. For example, I found out that Saint Solange at the age of seven gave her life to Christ, to become a servant of God most high.

In like manner as a Catholic child had my first communion and surrendered my life to Christ and committed myself to His service. My dedication to this vow increased over the years. Saint Solange cared for the sick, according to some accounts. Once again, I said "It can't be! How incredible!" I have taken care of the sick all of my working life. First, as a Nursing Assistant in the preemie nursery at Misericordia (now Mercy) Hospital in New York. Then in my professional life as a Registered Nurse. In fact, I have been a Nurse for nearly forty five years. I am now the owner of a nursing home caring for over 200 residents all of whom are sick or disabled. "How could this be?" That a girl who was born in 863 and I, who was born in the 1940's, have the same name and share so much in common.

By the time I looked up from my laptop, it was daybreak. There was no way I could sleep now. I was driven to search for more information about this mysterious Saint Solange. As I continued my online search I found that this girl, who only lived to the age of sixteen, was the one who literally cared for her family. "How could this be?" I was asking myself this question each time I read something that brought the two of us closer and closer. Once again, I confided to myself that the information that was revealing itself in different internet sites was exciting, overwhelming and now was beginning to feel like an overload of information and emotions. Just like Saint Solange, I have been carrying my entire family, literally and figuratively on my back for as long as I can remember. Skeptically, I challenged the facts before me. "There is no way this could be true."

By this time, goose pimples had spread from all over my arms to behind my neck as a chill ran down my back. Have you ever experienced a moment where you felt that you were not alone? I felt that way momentarily. However I was not frightened. I was just aware that something divine and marvelous was happening to me and I couldn't let go. I felt myself becoming more intense, more curious and more demanding of the nature of the supernatural forces that were participating in this connection. "Who is this girl?" "Does she now want me to know her?" "Is all this real or am I in the process of losing my mind?"

Our connection continued to reveal itself as I read. This young girl was a shepherdess who loved to care for the sheep. As a matter of fact, the beheaded pictures of Saint Solange on the internet

portray her with a sheep. "Here we go again" This girl and I also shared a love for animals. As a child growing up in Haiti, I had dogs, goats, pigeons, ducks and to date I still have a dog, that I love.

As I continued with my reading and research, I learned that Solange worked the land as a means to help support her family. I too, love to garden. I love it so much that my late husband used to say, I could not wait for the seasons to change, so I could go outside and work the land in my garden. My neighbors over the years have regularly come to the front yard of my Washington DC home with cameras to take pictures of my turtle garden. Every year at my home in Florida I tilled the soil and tended to the bananas, papayas, lemons, limes, bell peppers, beans and herb garden.

Now in what seems like a trance, I turned off my computer and closed my laptop to collect my thoughts. I wondered out loud could it be possible that this girl was somehow living in me? I saw that she died at the age of sixteen from blunt trauma. Could it be possible that due to the fact that she died so young, that God connected her spirit to mine? Yet if that were true, what would be the grand purpose behind it? I was once again questioning my own thoughts. I had heard about transference of spirits and wondered could something like that have happened to me? Could this old spirit still be alive and living in me? How strange!

For a short while I put my findings and feelings about Saint Solange on pause. I again felt overwhelmed. I thought if I tried to share this mysterious discovery with others, they might think I was suffering from a mental disorder. It did not take long however for the impulse to return. I was back on my computer, and resumed working on this project.

With my upbringing in Catholicism, my innate sense of curiosity and the inward sensation of a force pulling me deeper into the mystery of Saint Solange, I poured myself into researching and learning all the aspects of my mysterious new friend.

I wanted to know all about the making of a saint. Especially those involving women and even more so cephalophores, the decapitated saints who are depicted walking, talking or preaching while holding on to their heads. This was a phenomenon I found was not that unusual in France during the middle ages. I wanted to know how the church chooses saints and how Saint Solange fit the criteria.

I discovered that by the year 100 AD, Christians were honoring other Christians who had been martyred and asking for their intercession. The early Church believed that only the Christian who followed Christ perfectly would go immediately into the heavenly Jerusalem. Since perfection was conformity to Christ in life and in death, a process begun at baptism, the martyr (literally a witness) for Christ was seen to have achieved the goal. Thus, during the age of persecution (from Pentecost to about 311 AD) esteem for those Christians who had been killed because of their devotion and manifestation of faith, led Christians to extol their example as heroic

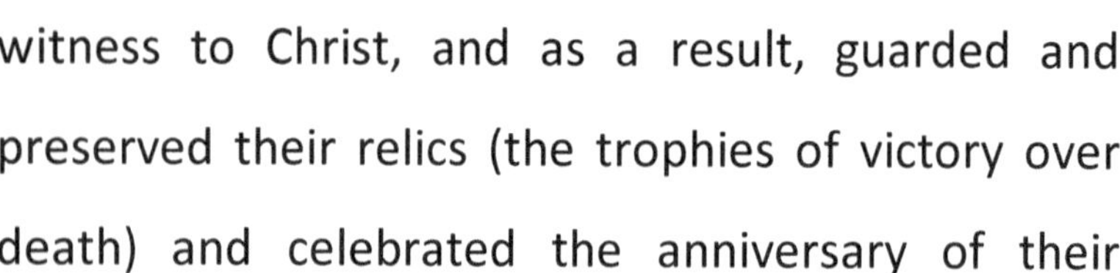

witness to Christ, and as a result, guarded and preserved their relics (the trophies of victory over death) and celebrated the anniversary of their death as a birthday to eternal life.

Honoring saints, as my research revealed to me, was a part of Christianity from the very beginning. As a matter of fact, this practice came from a long standing tradition in the Jewish faith of honoring prophets and holy people with shrines. The first saints were martyrs such as the apostles, John the Baptist and others who surrendered their lives for their faith in Jesus Christ.

In my attempt to research the route Saint Solange possibly traveled to sainthood, I became intrigued with the process and traced it to its present day, marveling at the historically significant changes. I learned that canonization the formal

process the Church used to name a saint was instituted around the 10th century. The first papal canonization was of St. Udalricus in 973.

To help clarify the canonization process, I was able to find in my research a Dr. Dustin Booher, a librarian at Catholic University in Washington DC, who among other things said, "For hundreds of years, starting with the first martyrs of the early Church, saints were chosen by public acclaim, which usually meant their virtue and miracles accredited to them were witnessed and acclaimed by the local archdiocese and bishops." The making of a saint thus originated on the local levels springing spontaneously from the will of the populace and that of special interest groups such as a bishop. Most often this informal process did not provide an opportunity for any kind of judicial investigation. In

the first eight or nine centuries, there was no centralized process for the canonization of a saint. Instead sainthood depended on popular affirmation or "spontaneous local attribution." At this point I believed that Solange must have been canonized by the acclamation of the people of Bourges. It wasn't until the 10th century that the formal process evolved and became truly centralized. Pope Sixtus V established the Congregation of Causes of Saints in 1588.

Although the informal approach appeared more democratic, eventually the Vatican took over the authority for approving saints. While, the age of martyrs has never truly ended, the relative cessation of murdering Christians that existed after the 4th century, meant martyrdom was no longer just the standard of perfection established for achieving sainthood. The Catholic Church started considering other models of holiness and procedures to confer canonization, ways in which conformity to Christ and a surrendered life could be a witness to the faithful and the world. This testimony was found in those who became disciples whose lifestyles exemplified to all the victory over sin and Christ's power over satan. Thus, those whose lives shone with examples of holiness began to enter the sacred sanctum of the canonized.

I had to stop, catch my breath and get a glass of water. The internet was enabling me to travel from the 16th century to the 20th century in seconds and discover in 1983, Pope John Paul II continued the process and made sweeping changes in the canonization procedure. The process now begins after the death of the Catholic person who people

regard as holy. Often the process starts many years after the death in order to give perspective on the candidate. The local bishop investigates the candidate's life and writings for heroic virtue (or martyrdom) and orthodoxy of doctrine. Then a panel of theologians and cardinals of the Congregation for the Causes of Saints and recognized by the Pope, they are called Venerable Servants of God. Beatification is the next step and requires evidence of one miracle (except in the case of martyrs). That would mean that Saint Solange would have been eligible for beatification even under the new guidelines. Since miracles are considered proof that the person is in heaven and can intercede for us, the miracle must take place after the candidate's death and as a result of a specific petition to the candidate. When the Pope proclaims the candidate beatified or "blessed," the

person can be venerated by a particular region or group of people with whom the person holds special importance.

The Vatican rules call for the final process of canonizing a saint only after two miracles can be properly affirmed, which includes martyrs as well. The title of saint tells us that the person lived a holy life, is in heaven and is to be honored by the universal Church. Canonization does not "make" a person a saint it recognizes what God has already done.

I also learned that even in the Catholic Church there can be exceptions to every rule. Yes, even the rules for canonization have exceptions. For example, the "two miracles" rule apparently was waived in the case of the popular Pope John Paul II who died April 2, 2005 and was canonized on April

27, 2014. This was one of the fastest canonizations in modern history. There was a controversy over whether or not a second miracle could be attributed to the intercession of Pope John Paul II. The current Pope Francis however, made an exception to the rule and signed a decree accepting one miracle as confirmation that Pope John Paul II should be canonized based on his holiness and life's work. More recently Pope Francis has made another exception by advancing Mother Teresa for canonization who died in 1997 at 87 years of age. I have been a follower of Mother Teresa's life and believe she was an extraordinary human being. I was especially elated when she was recognized by the world during her lifetime by being awarded the Nobel Peace Prize for her work helping the poor in Calcutta, India. However, back to the exception, normally there is a five year waiting period before

the initiation of the sainthood process, but Pope John Paul II waived it through special dispensation in 1999 and beatified her in 2003, the first step to sainthood. As stated earlier, two miracles validated by the Vatican are generally required for canonization and the prolific nun met both of them.

The first validated miracle attributed to Mother Teresa came after the Vatican concluded that an Indian woman's prayers to the nun caused her incurable tumor to disappear. This resulted in the beatification of Mother Teresa in 2003. The second miracle involved a Brazilian man who suffered a viral brain infection that cause multiple abscesses that eventually left him in a coma, dying. The ailing man's wife had been praying for months to Mother Teresa and on December 9, 2008, as he was about to be taken to emergency surgery, she and her husband's priest and relatives increased their prayers.

The next morning, the man fully awoke with normal brain function, according to a New York Times article. The man did not need surgery and resumed his work as a mechanical engineer. Moreover, although the doctors had previously told him that he was sterile because of his weakened immune system and antibiotics, he and his wife had two healthy children in 2009 and 2012. Recently a medical commission "voted unanimously that cure is incomprehensible in the light of present day medical knowledge." In addition, a theological inquiry voted unanimously that there was a perfect connection of cause and effect between the invocation of Mother Teresa and the scientifically inexplicable healing. This cleared the way for her canonization as early as 2016, according to the Vatican.

To many around the world Mother Teresa is already regarded as the people's saint. The order she founded, the Missionaries of Charity, a Roman Catholic congregation of women dedicated to helping the poor now has 4,000 members, operating in 100 nations.

Born on August 27, 1910, in Skopje, Macedonia, Mother Teresa taught in India for 17 years before she experienced her 1946 "call within a call" to devote herself to caring for the sick and the poor. Her order established a hospice, centers for the blind, aged, disabled and a leper colony. Since her death, people continue to seek her help and reportedly have experienced God's love for them through her prayers. Every day, pilgrims from

India and around the world come to pray at her tomb in Calcutta and many more follow her example of humble service of love to the sick and poorest of the poor.

Once again, it appears under the present rules Saint Solange could have been canonized, although the records of proof of miracles dating back to the 9th century would be more difficult to substantiate. However, as my research reveals canonization is infallible and irrevocable. While every person who is canonized is a saint, of course not every holy person has been canonized.

My research also cleared up a few of my misconceptions about sainthood. For instance, before my research, I used to think Catholics pray to saints and now I understand that, in reality we pray *with* saints, not to them. It is like asking someone

you trust, or understands your problems, someone close to God, to intercede for you on a particular issue. Since saints had to have lived lives of holiness and are now in heaven with Jesus, we feel their prayers are powerful in interceding for us.

The internet even enabled me to better understand the Bible, which shows many models of intercession. For example, many people have asked Saint Monica to pray for them when they have trouble with unanswered prayers, because Monica a 4th century saint, prayed for 20 years for her son to be converted. Eventually not only was he converted, her son Augustine went on to become a canonized saint as well. He is considered the father of Christian theology.

I also discovered many people involved in disasters pray to Saint Solange. For example, in

2011 people prayed that "the Lord Jesus, through the intercession of Saint Solange of Bourges, the Patron Saint against Drought," would come to the aid of the refugees fleeing famine, drought and violence in the Horn of Africa.

I firmly believe that in order for prayers to work one must also believe and have a strong faith that God not only hears us but answers us as well. Faith is not religion. Faith is trust and a knowing that the help we are seeking will come as a result of the faith in God. Faith requires patience and persistence. The answer to prayer does not always come when we want it but comes in its own time, because we do not control when we get the answer. Even so we must persist in prayer, which is our demonstration of faith. Thus, prayer and faith are intertwined.

All my life I have prayed and many times praying to my parents and grandparents because this was the way we were bought up in my family. My parents and the parents of Saint Solange, based on my reading believed in prayers. To date, you will hear my sisters and brothers invoke the name of our deceased parents, stating that prayer was one of the most valuable gifts they gave to all of us. We always feel protected by the spirits of our parents and grandparents. Although they were not saints, but they believed in prayer, taught us how to pray and for that we are grateful to them and continue to always pray for them.

When my late husband who promised me that we would grow old together suddenly died and left me to grow old alone, I asked Saint Anthony, the patron saint who helps the faithful to regain

their loss, to help me find a mate to replace my husband. A year after my husbands' death, I met Clifford who has been at my side ever since. He is the best Saint Anthony could have found for me. I believed in the prayer to Saint Anthony and he delivered. I know God answers prayers. This is at the heart of my Catholic faith.

As my research continued, I then discovered that Saint Solange is a patron saint. Indeed Saint Solange is the patron saint of many causes such as children, animals, rape and disasters such as drought. She is also the patron saint of Berry, France and Bourges, France. "How do saints become patron saints?" Internet and library research revealed that patron saints are selected as special protectors or guardians over specific areas of life. These areas include occupations, illnesses,

churches, countries and causes, encompassing anything that is important to us.

Early records show that people and churches started to be named after apostles and martyrs about the 4th century. More recently, even the popes have named patron saints. Patrons can also be chosen by individuals or groups as well. Patron saints are chosen often today because an interest, talent or event in their lives, overlaps with the special area. For instance, Saint Francis of Assisi loved nature and so he is patron saint of ecologists.

Saint Frances de Sales was a writer and so he is the patron saint of writers and journalists. Saint Clare of Assisi was named patron saint of television because on Christmas when she was too ill to leave her bed, she heard and saw Christmas mass on her wall, even though it was taking place miles away.

Angels can also be named patron saints. A patron saint can help us when we follow the example of that saint's intercessory prayers to God.

Saint Solange is listed as a patron saint of the worldwide organization Carmellian Task Force Servants of St. Camillus Disaster Relief Services (SCTF SOS DRS). As a patron saint, she is called upon to intervene in disasters because of the disastrous circumstance of her death. The group is part of an international disaster relief network of the Catholic Order of the Ministers of the Infirmed.

I also learned that in 2011, the Carmellian doctors prayed for Saint Solange to intervene in the impending drought facing 2.5 million people in Mexico. Prayers for the intervention of Saint Solange also included a bus accident in Switzerland

on March 13, 2012 and a drought in China in the winter of 2009.

As my research caused me to better understand the process of canonization, I also wanted to know if Saint Solange's gender had an effect on the selection process. I learned that the sainthood of women was not rare in the early establishment of the Christian Church. Although opposed by some, the Church's commitment to diversity was justified by scriptures such as Galatian 3:28 text, "There is neither Jew nor Greek, neither slave or free, neither male nor female; for you are all one in Christ Jesus."

Despite the traditional barriers to gender equality, the spread of Christianity during the sixth century, especially in the northern regions of Europe, new opportunities opened up for women.

Women deemed living lifestyles of holiness along with those of power and wealth were recruited to establish churches, monasteries and educational centers. Many became strong charismatic figures within their religious communities. Their essential roles in the establishment of Christianity led to their visibility and recognition, eventually leading to sainthood. Thus during this initial period, the validation of women was translated into a record numbers of saints. As I discovered, about 1 out of every 3 saints were female. These numbers drastically declined as time went on.

Women commemorated as saints from these early centuries include several martyrs who suffered under the persecution of Christians in the Roman Empire, such as Agnes of Rome, Saint Cecilia and Agatha of Sicily. In late Antiquity, Saint Helena,

was a Christian and the mother of Emperor Constantine I. As such, her role in history is of great significance considering her son Constantine legalized Christianity across the Roman Empire and converted as well. Constantine ended centuries of mistreatment of Christians, changing the culture of world history.

Similarly, Saint Monica was a pious Christian and the mother of Saint Augustine of Hippo who, after being a wayward youth, converted to Christianity. St. Augustine went on to become one of the most influential Christian theologians of all history. In addition, to my own Saint Solange.

It became clear that I was spending an incredible number of hours, days and weeks researching, tracking and even in a positive sense, stalking Saint Solange. She came into my life as a

mystery and was progressively becoming my soul mate. The more I learned about her, the more I wanted to learn, not only about her but also the how, the what and the where. Is it possible to meet someone in the spirit, without ever physically seeing them? I had heard of ghosts chasing people, well, was I chasing a ghost? Or was a ghost chasing me?

Although, I felt I was reaching the saturation point with my paper and internet pursuit. My faithful and consistent online searching could not satisfy my hunger for the revelation of Solange. This woman who had been deceased for centuries had now taken up residency in my heart. For a few months, I had been tantalized by the hors d'oeuvre, now the *entrée* the main course must be next. The more I thought about the next steps, the odder

some of the circumstances surrounding the saint seemed to me. Why was it that although I had traveled to France multiple times, I had never heard of Bourges where the saint was born? Nor had I heard about the chapel or the church that bore her name. Once I learned that there was both a chapel and church named after Saint Solange, I found new energy. My inner engine cranked up and I became a ball of motion. Now, I had a location and a church, something concrete to find. That was certainly progress made.

My desperate need for more information motivated me to call the church in Bourges that was associated with the Chapel of Saint Solange. I placed the call but then had great difficulty understanding the person on the other end of the phone because of her strong French accent. Even though I grew up speaking and was educated in French, after being in the United States since the mid-1960's made understanding this woman quite the challenge. All my education since immigrating to the US from Haiti has been in English.

My professional work has been conducted in English. However, most communication with my family is done in Creole (a Haitian dialect). At this point, I must admit that my French is far from perfect. I can carry a conversation with mistakes along the way but my conversation with the church assistant in Bourges was not at all successful. We had great deal of difficulty understanding and communicating with each other.

I could not let the language barrier defeat me and soon realized I had family in France that I could reach out to. This new found family started in 2000

with a letter from a woman in France who claimed she had found me on the internet while she was researching her family genealogy. She told me that her name was Josiane Vivens and she believed we were related. Enclosed in the letter was a picture of Josiane and her husband Jacques. It was obvious that she was as white as I am black. She also provided me with a map of the family tree she had created based on her research. Josiane's letter started its own adventure in family and friendship.

My cousin Josiane and I at Saint Solange Church

As the years went by, Josiane and I continued to communicate via the internet, phone and letters which included exchanging pictures. We were both excited about meeting and eventually she came to Washington DC to visit me, her new family.

I contacted every Vivens descendant I could find and invited them to the welcome party for Josiane and Jacques at my home in Washington DC. Josiane and Jacques came with an abundance of

gifts for all the people they were hoping to meet. The gift they included for me was a bottle of French wine. To my surprise it was labeled with the name Vivens, from a Vivens winery in Bordeaux, France. This is yet another story to be shared in another book. Unbeknownst to Josiane, I had assembled many family members that she did not know, love and goodwill was her gift to all who were present at the party.

From Vivens Winery

As part of the genealogy that Josiane shared, I learned we are descendants of three French brothers. One of the brothers, an engineer was sent to Haiti during the French possession of Haiti to build roads and bridges. In Haiti, he married a black woman and started a family into which I was later

born. Josiane is the descendant of one of the other two brothers and one of whom is somewhat attached to the winery that bears the Vivens name.

Over the years I have visited Josiane in France and she has returned to Washington DC to visit her black family as we affectionately call each other.

Years ago, learning that I had French relatives was quite a shock, but now I believe they were positioned for this very moment, to assist me in this divine assignment. I felt Josiane's discovery of me was an act of God bringing us together, in preparation for bringing Saint Solange of Bourges into my life. I wondered again why me? Why now? Why did it take so long for me to know that there was a Saint Solange? I am in church all the time. I read religious books. I know several priest and they

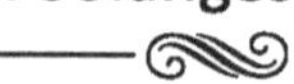

know me by name. In all these years, how come no one ever told me there was a Saint Solange?

As time went on, I confess, I was becoming obsessed. I wanted to connect the dots. Maybe I was possessed, which is a good thing as long as one is possessed by God. There were so many pieces that needed to be pulled together. Now with my French connection I felt that with God's help, I could fit all of the pieces together.

I was so happy to be able to reach out to my French cousin Josiane and her husband Jacques, to assist me with my research. I texted Jacques and explained my recent discovery of Saint Solange and requested his assistance in my search for more information about the Saint that I was starting to think of as my twin. Jacques quickly responded that

he was going to do his best to complete the research.

It was not long before he sent me all the information I needed. With Jacques assistance, I learned that Saint Solange had her own church and a village named after her. He also confirmed that she had her own chapel as well.

Although my communication efforts with the church in Bourges failed because of the language barrier, I still wanted to keep moving forward. Jacques sent me the phone number of the person that I needed to contact at the Saint Solange Church in the village.

There is a six hour difference in time between the United States and France. So, I had to wait from the time I received Jacques correspondence and the

right time to call Saint Solange Church. As I waited to make the call, I worried the whole time whether the strong French accent on the other end would once again be a deterrent to our communication.

To my surprise, this time I had less difficulty understanding the lady from Saint Solange Church in the village in comparison to the person in Bourges that I had spoken to previously. It had become easier for me after reading so much information and speaking to Jacques and Josiane in French. I was becoming more fluent in the spoken language.

The more I read and the more I talked to my cousin, the more I became convinced that I had to travel to Saint Solange the village, where this saint had lived. After all, this saint had taken up residency in my being; she had become a tenant in my mind. I

had become convinced that my footsteps were being led by God. I was being called to do what was still a mystery to me. I had been walking on an intuitive path ever since I accidently discovered the existence of this saint. At this point this was more than a passing fancy; it was a compulsion, something I just had to do.

As I continued on my journey, it looked like my life and that of Saint Solange continued to intersect at every corner. It seemed that each new development would just energize me to not miss a step and to keep moving forward. What a surprise it was to find out that the feast of Saint Solange is celebrated annually on May the 10th. What makes this so remarkable is that the day of her death which is also considered her birthday into eternal life is also my birthday. Saint Solange is also

celebrated on Pentecostal Monday which in 2015 fell on May 25th. That also has special meaning to me because I am also celebrated twice in the month of May. Now, these two celebrations of Saint Solange had an even deeper meaning for me. Once again what was happening around this saint was also mimicking my life or…my life was mimicking hers since she was my senior by a few centuries.

My whole family and friends in Haiti are aware that I was born May 10th. All my birthday parties since infancy to the day that I entered the United States of America were on May the 10th. However, all that changed when I got my passport to come to the United States. In Haiti, back in those days, as a child you were not allowed to ever touch your birth certificate. When there was a need for your birth certificate to be used mainly for school

registration, your parents would take the birth certificate to the school and have you registered.

The birth certificate is considered a precious document that was to be protected and was always in the custody of your parents, under lock and key.

When I received my passport from the immigration office to travel to the United States in the mid 1960's, I learned that on my birth certificate, used by the immigration officer to complete my passport, it shows my date of birth as May the 11th, not May the 10th! I was flabbergasted, angry and confused as to what this would mean to my travel arrangements. I confronted my parents on the discrepancy and they admitted to never having paid attention to what was written on the birth certificate, but reassured me that I was born on May 10th. Thus, every year, my family calls and

sends me birthday cards, gifts and flowers on May 10th. However, all my American acquaintances celebrate my birthday on May 11th. I used to jokingly tell people, I was the only Solanges whose birthday is celebrated twice. Now, how *amazing* is that?

I consider this another intersection of kinship. The connection Saint Solange and I have, some would call a coincidence, but I call it divine intervention that continues to intertwine me with Saint Solange.

When I think about my trip to France, I recalled asking the lady on the phone, from Saint Solange Church, which event she recommended I attend. She replied, and I will translate her comments in English, "If I were you, I would come to the Pentecostal Monday celebration because, we

have a major procession with all the children. The Archbishop of Bourges and hundreds of people from all over the world come and participate. I really think you should come then." My comprehension of French was getting much better.

I was overjoyed that Saint Solange was also celebrated on Pentecostal Monday. As I recall from my early lessons about the church, Pentecost is a very important celebration. Since the first century, Pentecost Sunday is often called Whit Sunday in certain European countries. It is also one of the most sacred observances in Christendom. Pentecost commemorates the Holy Spirit's post-Resurrection visit to the apostles in the upper room in Jerusalem. It also marks the birth of the Christian Church. Like Pentecost, Whit Monday is movable because it is determined by the Easter date. Whit

Monday, Pentecost Monday is celebrated as a holiday in many European counties. In France the entire Pentecostal week used to be a holiday but after the 1789 French Revolution, only Monday remained a public holiday. Whit Monday also gets its name from the white clothes usually worn for Baptism.

Pentecostal Monday is also a major event in the history of Saint Solange for another reason; after the brutal death of Solange, the faithful of Saint Martin-du-Crot Church, took charge of her body and buried her at the site where she was murdered. Subsequently, the Church of Saint Martin-du-Crot burned down and was rebuilt as it is today. Then on June 8th, 1511 which was Pentecostal Monday, the Saint Martin-du-Crot Church was renamed and dedicated to Saint

Solange. Her bones were given to the church and to date; those relics are suspended in a reliquary in Saint Solange Church. As part of the celebration, her relics are taken down every year on Pentecostal Monday and in a mile long procession, they are carried from Saint Solange Church in the province of Berry to Saint Solange Chapel for a second celebration.

Saint Solange Church

"Amazing!" With this new information, I declared, "no more procrastination or hesitation, I'm going to France!" That was it! Case closed! My visit to Saint Solange could not be put off any longer. I had to go now because next year would be too late. I could not imagine spending another year dealing with my yearning to see Bourges. From my discovery of Saint Solange in the latter part of the

month of February, I became certain that my trip was imminent by mid-April, which meant that I had to move fast and make all of my arrangements. I had just two weeks to pull everything together. The big decision was which celebration should I attend? I wanted to attend mass at Saint Solange Church on May 10th. My birthday mass celebration is a ritual that I do every year. Combining that with Saint Solange's celebration would be awesome! I was also curious about the big celebration on Pentecostal Monday. Finally, I made the big decision...I decided to attend both celebrations.

With the big decision made, I called Josiane and Jacques to tell them the news. They immediately offered to pick me up at the Charles de Gaulle Airport in Paris and extended an invitation to stay with them for the next fifteen days. This included driving me to Bourges, for mass on May 10th and again on May 25th, Pentecostal Monday for the Saint Solange Procession. I felt excited and blessed.

As an entrepreneur, I was not impeded by having to ask my boss for time off from work and fortunately I also did not have any financial roadblocks usually associated with taking off for a month. I felt a curious mix of excitement, anxiety and inner turmoil about launching off into the unknown. Although I was not venturing off as a tourist or sightseer gathering tokens and postcards, I was searching for a soul connection and a spiritual bond with a person I discovered on the internet.

Not to mention, this person had been deceased for 12 centuries. Yet I was in awe of this person. A bond had somehow formed between us

and it was strong enough to summon me across oceans and time zones, going from one continent to another.

Would my findings settle this longing? Was I chasing a fantasy or fairytale? Would the trip add deeper meaning and purpose to my own life experience? My head was spinning. There were those who were questioning my impulsive behavior. I had others who wished to be in my shoes. There were still others who offered to join me if I would pay for their trip.

Finally, all the plans had been made and tickets purchased. The next chapter in this incredible journey was about to begin. The time for contemplation was coming to an end. The time for taking off was drawing near.

On May 8th, I started the physical part of my journey, taking a US Air flight from Reagan National Airport in Washington to Boston. It connected with an American Airline flight from Boston to Paris. Unfortunately, but not unusual, the flight leaving Reagan National Airport had a long departure delay that threatened my Boston connection. I became very anxious over the possibility of missing my flight to Paris. To me this would have been disastrous. Missing this flight meant missing my May 10th birthday mass in Saint Solange Church which was one of the main goals of my trip. All this work and planning would have been in vain. The flight from Virginia to Boston was a very short flight, however because of our late departure we arrived in Boston with only 20 minutes left for me to reach the American Airlines terminal. To aggravate matters in the worst way, the door to the aircraft had

difficulties opening. This just added to my delay in reaching my connection. I made it clear to the other first class passengers that I absolutely had to be the very first person to leave the plane in order to make my connecting flight.

The flight attendant told me we were at gate 19, but my connecting flight was leaving from gate 46! The last thing I wanted to hear was anything negative, but there it was. One man who over-heard the flight attendant stated "you will never make it." Another man stated, "there is a shortcut and if you run, you still have a chance." His encouragement and explanation of the shortcut put an extra leap in my step. I took off like an Olympian sprinter in the race of her life, making sure that I followed the shortcut directions that were given to me.

As I ran past the magazine racks and the fast food kiosks, I yelled out along the way, "where is gate 46?" Someone shouted back and pointed "straight ahead." Once that was confirmed, I ran even faster. I had no carryon to pull, carrying only my backpack strapped to my body. I ran for more than a mile, from gate 19 to gate 46. I barely made the flight. I got there just before the American Airlines aircraft door closed. I had prayed along the way to Saint Solange for her help in not letting me miss the flight. When I found my seat on the plane taking me from Boston to Charles de Gaulle Airport, it took over an hour for my nerves to settle down. My legs and feet were shaking. I could certainly feel the pain. The strain I imposed on this 60+ year old body with the non-stop run through the airport was excruciating. Nevertheless, I finally got comfortable and breathed a sigh of relief when the plane finally

took off. As soon as it was available I had a nice drink, good food and positioned my seat to get relaxed and rested.

It was a six hour flight, however I must have fallen asleep instantly because, after what seemed like a minute after getting comfortable, I was startled awake by the announcement to fasten our seatbelts in preparation for landing.

I had programmed my watch to register time changes and saw it was the early morning of May 9th. Completing the second leg of my journey, I had high hopes that the rest of my trip would be less nerve-racking than what I had experienced earlier.

Unfortunately my anxieties resurfaced when I arrived at the baggage area and could not find my luggage even after waiting patiently. Suitcases, boxes, golf clubs and all kinds of sporting equipment circled around the carousel, arriving in the hands of their owners. However, none of that belonged to me. I saw what looked like the last bag coming off the carousel. Nothing was behind it so I had to accept the fact that although I made it to the plane, my bags apparently had not traveled as fast. Coming to the conclusion that my bags did not make it, I went on to look for Josiane and Jacques fearing they would leave once they saw all the Boston passengers exiting the airport and I did not appear.

What joy I felt when I spotted my cousin Josiane and her husband Jacques. I hugged and held them for a long time. It had been a few years since we had seen each other. Then I broke the news that my bags did not make it to Paris. Jacques

immediately took charge of the situation. He knew exactly where to take me for a declaration of lost luggage. After completing all the pertinent papers, we made arrangements with the airline to deliver my bags to Jacques and Josiane's home on the afternoon of Monday, May 11th since we were heading to Bourges for the weekend.

Soon we were on our way. First, to their home in Gif-sur-Yvette, a province of France, outside of Paris. We drove through the spellbindingly beautiful countryside to the city of Bourges. The ancient city of Bourges can be traced all the way back to the 5th century BC. It is now home to approximately 100,000 inhabitants with room for growth and expansion. It covers an area which is almost two-thirds that of Paris. However, unlike Paris, Bourges is complete with marshes that

are found in protected wetlands and new gardens abound. The cultural life of the city boomed from 1963 when the *Maison de la Culture* was opened. Nearby, the Congress Centre (completed in 1983), the Natural History Museum (completely renovated in 1989) can be found grouped together.

Bourges even had university campus development in the 1990's with the Faculties of Science and Law, the Chamber of Commerce Training Centre and the Ecole Nationale Supérieure d'Ingénieurs de Bourges (School of Higher Engineering). This completes the University Institute of Technology (1968) and the National School of Fine Arts which is located in the restored former Jesuit college. Bourges has succeeded in growing into modern times, without destroying its rich history.

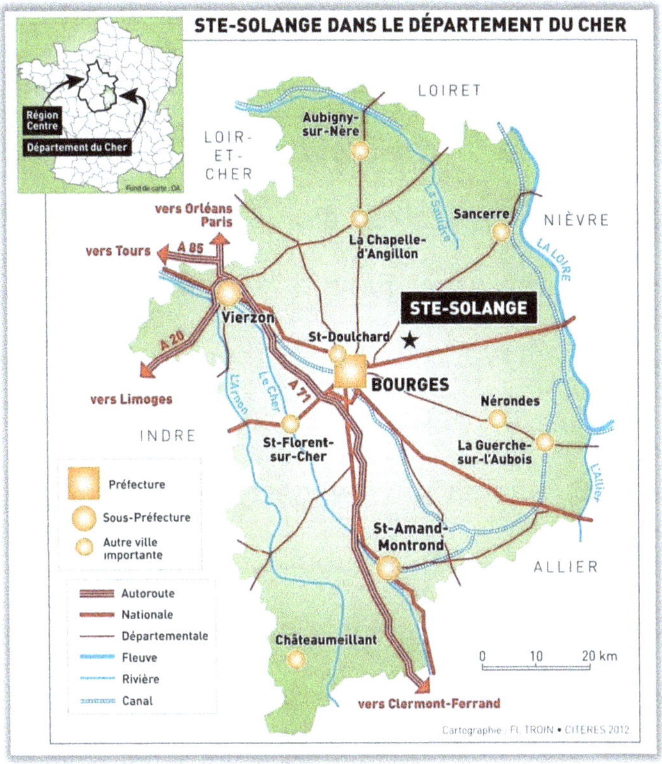

Map of Bourges

Arriving at Bourges was breathtaking. However, the streets are so narrow. On the one hand I felt like the walls of the building were closing in on me as we walked along, viewing the historic sights. On the other hand, I felt like I was stepping into a dream world that even though, I had strained to imagine it, the reality was, I could not have imagined this in my wildest of dreams. I was overwhelmed with emotion and had to stop to catch my breath. Just a few months before, I had no idea this historic figure named Saint Solange even existed. Now, here I was within walking distance, steps away from entering her church. How mind boggling was that?

After getting familiar with our new surroundings, we made our way to our hotel. It was Saturday and I needed to prepare to attend Saint

Solange Church for Sunday service. While checking into the hotel, we asked the concierge for their closest mall. In addition to giving us great directions, she also added one more pertinent detail, the stores in Bourges closed for the day at 6:30 pm. It was already 5:30 pm in the evening. To my dismay, we only had one hour for me to get what I needed for the weekend since I had no clothes and only a few personal items in my backpack.

Once again a mad dash was required. Thank goodness this time I had Josiane and Jacques to race around with me. We were running like crazy people from shop to shop. I had so much to buy and so little time. I needed shoes, suitable church clothes, sleepwear, underwear and other personal items. I spent seven hundred and fifty dollars in less

than an hour! I never thought I could shop so fast and spend so much money in so little time! We were each the last customer in different stores at the same time. There was no time to bargain, which I love to do. I only had time to find what I thought would fit, grab it and pay just before the doors closed.

We returned to the hotel, dropped off the many shopping bags and strolled to a nearby bistro for dinner. I was again bubbling with excitement from the rush of shopping and the realization that I was finally here at the place I anticipated would unlock the mystery of Saint Solange to me. I felt overwhelmed, in awe and exhausted.

After dinner, we strolled slowly to Bourges Cathedral to see a festival of lights. A show that was illuminated brilliance. We discovered, each evening

at this time of year, the lights on the Cathedral change into different breath-taking colors. An ancient church colored in festive lights. It was beautiful. Lots of people were taking pictures and I could hear the expressions of disbelief at the majestic beauty each time the Cathedral changed into a different color. I had to pinch myself to confirm I was not dreaming. I said out loud, "What a wonderful greeting." It was perfect. I concluded that the Cathedral was an excellent tourist attraction and made it a point to return for a visit during the day on my next trip to Bourges.

Early Sunday morning, we had breakfast at the hotel and then drove for a half an hour to Saint Solange village. The little village was quainter than the city of Bourges and arresting in its beauty. Most of the homes were small and well maintained

singles houses, surrounded by miles of greenery full of lush grass, vegetation and trees. We arrived at an intersection where there was an arrow pointing to the right, the direction of Saint Solange Chapel. There was another arrow pointing to the left the direction of Saint Solange Church. Since we were early for mass, Jacques suggested that we drive to the chapel. For a moment, I had to bring myself to a halt, just to mull over what I was thinking and feeling. Just a few weeks ago, I was at my home in Washington DC, I never thought I would ever be confronted with such astonishing choices. Yet, here I was thousands of miles from home standing at the intersection of two very real places that until now had been figments of my imagination. Turn to the right or go to the left? To have such a choice, to even be here. I rubbed my eyes and blinked...what a dream come true.

I decided we would turn right towards the chapel. From the moment we made the right turn, there were no houses in sight. On both sides of the narrow street and as far as the eyes could see, there were vast open spaces of greenery. About a mile down the road, there was a sudden shift.

Saint Solange Chapel

A small building came into view on the left. Jacques screamed; "There it is!" As Josiane and I turned our heads to the left, we saw a little chapel deep at the end of a long narrow dirt road. The green radiance of the leaves on the trees cascaded in majestic beauty on both sides.

"Stop the car," I said and then I let out a scream. At that electrifying moment nothing could have restrained my joy or held me back! This is what I had waited for. I wanted to run down the road to the chapel, but I remembered my exhaustion from the run through the airport and restricted myself to a brisk walk. "I'm here! I'm here!" I was in awe. In order to hold on to the moment, I pulled out my iPad to take a video and began to narrate the experience. Saint Solange Chapel is very old. The wood door is in desperate

need of painting. I turned the handle to enter, but it was locked.

There was no inscription on the small dilapidated building. There was however the silhouette of Saint Solange with her sheep above the chapel door. In addition there was a flyer taped to the door announcing her celebration on Monday, May 25th.

As we walked the grounds, I noted all the renovation work that needed to be done on the site. The centuries had taken their toll on this small chapel. Several of the stained glass windows were broken, many areas of the wall were peeling and mold was visible around the window panes. I also noticed the roof was in desperate need of repair as well.

Solange Chapel Window

Nevertheless, all the deterioration had not spoiled or overwhelmed my discovery. It was like visiting a beloved elderly aunt and looking beyond

the wrinkles on her face, to appreciate the beauty and grace her life had brought to so many throughout the years. In fact, in the back of my mind I wondered, was the fading state of the chapel, the raison d'être that I was here standing on hallowed ground.

Lost in thought, I could probably have stayed at the chapel for many more hours, to drink in the essence of what I was seeing and feeling. I had thought about the chapel, read about it, but now to be standing here filled me completely with gratitude to God. "Thank you God," I said out loud. No one could have made this possible but God. However even in that moment I was shaken from my reverie. It was time to go on to our other sacred occasion. Onward we went to Saint Solange Church

for the 11 o'clock mass on my birthday, Sunday, May 10th.

We arrived at Saint Solange Church before most of the other churchgoers. Before long however, all the pews were filled. I first surveyed the crowd, of which there were about seventy five people in total. Then I took a good look at my surroundings. I noticed that although the church was small and very, very old, it was clean and well maintained in comparison to Saint Solange Chapel. The difference in the state of the chapel, compared to the church, caused me to wonder if the chapel was utilized for anything other than for the Saint Solange celebration on Pentecostal Monday.

As we settled into our pew, a stocky, elderly, yet kind-looking gentleman appeared from the vestibule of the church. He was dressed in a black

suit and had a small cross pinned to the lapel of his suit jacket. He made his way through the congregation, greeting each attendee, one by one. When he approached me, I introduced myself and explained the reason for my visit, he gave me a curious look. I thought, I might have appeared out of place, since I was the only person of color in the church on that day. However, he was very kind. He held my hand and welcomed me to Saint Solange Church.

I was seated in the front row, close to the altar. A church bulletin noted that the altar was erected in 1281. As I gazed to my left, I noticed I was seated a few feet away from an almost life sized statue of Saint Solange adorned in all white. To my right was the headless statue of Saint Solange that I had first seen on the internet and in

the books I had acquired while conducting my research.

Now I was a few feet away and as I looked at the headless statue I became mesmerized. A tingling sensation passed through my body and I felt a deep longing to make Saint Solange a part of my life. As I looked above the statue of Saint Solange, I saw hanging on the wall, a beautiful statue of the Virgin Mary, the Mother of God, whom I adore.

While I was sitting there before the service began, I started to think about Saint Solange and headless saints in general. I had uncovered on the internet that there are quite a few headless saints and martyrs. Legend states that after Saint Solange was beheaded, she picked up her head, called out

to Jesus three times and walked to the St. Martin-du-Crot Church where she later died.

Some may say that the story of Saint Solange is hard to believe, but not me. First, miracles are extraordinary events caused by God. From the Immaculate Conception to the Resurrection, to the parting of the Red Sea and hundreds of other Biblical miracles all require faith to believe in them. Secondly, there are also a number of decapitated martyrs noted to have communicated after being beheaded. There are many decapitated martyrs who picked up their heads and proceeded to speak or pray. The word Cephalophores was actually created to describe the phenomenon; it is derived from the Greek word meaning head carriers. From the internet and various books I learned that historically, there are hundreds of cephalophores,

with more than 100 from France alone, according to Mike Culpepper who wrote a blog on the subject.

Examples of cephalophoric saints who were decapitated because of their commitment to Christ abound. For example, Saint Nicasius of Rheims, France was martyred in the early 5th century. He was said to have been reciting Psalm 119, as he was decapitated. As he reached the verse; "Adhaesit pavimento anima mea"-"My soul is attached onto dust", he was executed. He then continued reciting "Vivifica me Domino secundum verbum tuum"-"Revive me Lord, with your words", even after his head had fallen to the ground. He is sometimes depicted in art, walking with the upper part of his head and its miter in his hand. Saint Nicasius was part of the movement that helped establish France's Christian roots that hold firm today. A

Benedictine abbey in Rheims, France was later named in his honor.

Examples of the decapitated speaking head can also be found in Southern France. In Beziers in Southern France, there is the legend of Saint Aphrodisius, an Egyptian who was martyred in Alexandria in the 1st century. As legend has it, Aphrodisius was preaching the Gospel, when a group of pagans pressed through the crowd and beheaded him on the spot. Aphrodisius picked up his head and carried it to a chapel which was recently consecrated and is identified today as Place Saint-Aphrodise, Beziers.

Among the well known female cephalophores is Saint Valerie of Limoges, a city in central France. She is a legendary Christian martyr whose cult (a system of religious veneration) was very important

in the medieval period. She has been an important subject for Christian art since the Middle Ages and for porcelain figurines over several centuries. The incident most consistently retold about Saint Valerie is that she was beheaded because of her faith in Christ and then carried her own head to set before her Bishop, Saint Martial who had converted her.

The most prominent of the cephalophores in French history is Saint Denis, the patron saint of Paris. In the 3rd century, he was Bishop of Paris. Denis and his companions were so effective in converting people to Christianity that the pagan priests became alarmed over their loss of followers. At their instigation, he was arrested. After a long imprisonment, Denis and two of his clergy were executed by beheading on the highest hill in Paris (now Monmartre). After being beheaded, Denis was said to have picked up his head and walked 10 kilometers (6 miles) from the summit of the hill, preaching a sermon the entire way. Of the many accounts of his martyrdom, this is noted in the Golden Legend and in Butler's Lives of Saints. The site where he stopped preaching and actually died was marked by a shrine that developed into the Saint Denis Basilica, which later became the burial place for kings of France. A 1317 illustrated manuscript depicting The Life of Saint Denis, once owned by King Phillip V of France, is preserved in the Bibliothèque Nationale in Paris.

To some scholars of Medieval French history the distinctive trait of cephalophory, where the severed head continues preaching or talking is not quite the abnormality it is to the rest of us. French

culture is fairly rich in these acts which were viewed as a powerful assertion of autonomy or perhaps, victory over death, in the face of persecution. The latter was exemplified by reports that Bishop Denis continued preaching for a short spell after his execution. In Saint Valerie's case, the severed head is returned to where it belongs, to the deceased person's bishop, pastor or confessor.

In Saint Solange's case, her ability to pick up her severed head and walk, points to the miraculous power of God in the lives of the faithful. This has lifted the hearts and minds of people for generations. In all these cases, there is a continuity in the relationship to Jesus and the church going beyond death and in a sense, through the miracle of heaven coming to earth.

A REVELATION

My mental relapse into my research was broken by the sound of the church bells announcing the 11 o'clock mass was finally starting. As I lifted my head and looked towards the altar, I realized the stocky elderly man who had greeted me earlier was now dressed as a priest and was proceeding to face the church as the celebrant of the mass.

As the mass started, I listened attentively trying to understand the French. It was difficult hearing and understanding the readings because of the strong French accents of the readers. Luckily the church had distributed a program with all the readings and songs for the mass. This was very helpful to me as I tried to follow and participate in the mass. When the priest spoke, I could actually understand him and really enjoyed the mass.

In the Catholic churches I attend in Washington DC, the priest usually announces the purpose of the celebration, at the beginning of the mass. To my joy, this mass was no different. There was however one major surprise… the priest announced that one of the purposes of this mass was to celebrate ME! In fact, his actual words were, "This mass is being celebrated for Saint Solange and for all the Solanges who are celebrating their birthday today, like our American Solanges, who flew in yesterday from the United States to be here with us and is celebrating her birthday as well today, with our Saint Solange." Oh no he didn't!, but yes, he did!

Upon the priests' introduction, everyone's heads turned around looking for this guest. I stood up, smiled and waved my hand to identify myself.

They smile and mass continued. When mass ended, many parishioner's came over and greeted me warmly.

You can't imagine how I felt. I was no longer thinking or dreaming about one day being in the church of Saint Solange. I was here. The priest connected Saint Solange and I, for the whole congregation to hear. I was not a stranger looking in from outside, through the stained glass window. I was actually inside, seeing and breathing it all in. I was again, overwhelmed with gratitude. I had to wipe away a tear.

To make matters even more phenomenal, a couple from the church came over, introduced themselves and invited us to lunch.

The couple took Josiane, Jacques and I to a quaint, little restaurant, with no more than a few tables. The restaurant had a set menu already prepared. The food, no matter how delicious, could not hold my attention. I wanted to know all about my new acquaintances and what they could tell me about Saint Solange and her chapel.

Jocelyn, the lady who invited us to lunch along with her husband Thierry, told me she was born in Saint Solange village. She confided that she was very attached to the Saint Solange Church and her husband managed the Saint Solange Chapel. I mentioned to her that we stopped at the chapel before attending the mass, but the doors were locked and we were not able to see the inside. Jocelyn's husband, who had been rather quiet but attentive throughout the entire lunch, stated in a

matter of fact tone, "It just so happens, that I have the key to the chapel in my pocket. I can take you there to see it after lunch if you wish."

"If I wish?" I definitely wish! What a surprise! No. Surprise was not the right word...downright shocked better describes my reaction. Some might call it a mere coincidence or accident but my thoughts went further than that. I wondered, in some mysterious way, had Saint Solange sent for me? Did she want me to see the inside of her chapel? How do you explain that with all the people that attended the mass, the one couple with the key to the chapel, are the ones who invited us to lunch? How do you explain that?

They did not know us and we did not know them. We were all complete strangers and yet

instantly connected by spirit. Was this the prelude of a Saint Solange miracle? How cool was this?

While we chatted like old friends over lunch, I could hardly sit still in my seat. Finally, Thierry, sensing my eagerness to see the inside of the chapel offered to take us there. Josiane, Jacques and I followed Thierry and Jocelyn's car, since we had no idea where we were. All I can remember seeing were dirt roads with tall, glorious bushes of vegetation on both sides.

As we approached the chapel, I remembered where I had been earlier. Like a child, again I could not wait to get out of the car and run inside. What an indescribable moment with, a truly indescribable feeling. How coincidental was that? Was this another act of God? I had learned of it, read about it, wished I could see it and now here we were.

Inside this little chapel were a few benches and a few different size statues of Saint Solange perched on several walls. The most striking one was a human size replica of Solange as a young girl with her head attached to her body. She was wearing a beautiful teal and white dress, lying in a glass case under the altar. When Solange was martyred she was sixteen years old and very beautiful. I stood motionless, staring and thinking how tragic it was for such a lovely life to be ended at such a young age, in such a barbaric way.

Jocelyn came up behind me and said, "We carry her body in the procession on Pentecostal Monday, from the church to the chapel and after the procession, she is placed back here, under the altar until next year."

Replica of Solange in Saint Solange Chapel

Then she asked, "Would you like to carry her during the procession?" How incredible, I thought to myself. "Yes," I said without hesitation. "I would love to carry her."

In the re-enactments of the Passion of the Cross, many of the faithful carry the heavy, wooden cross of Jesus. In like manner, this congregation carries the replica of young Solange, before her

martyrdom. This ritual has been commemorated for centuries every year on Pentecostal Monday. How great is that? We continued touring the quaint little chapel, going upstairs to a balcony that opened to the front. There I was told that in previous years, the priest would stand on the balcony to address the congregation below prior to the mass that followed the procession. Consistent with the outside of the chapel, the inside of the chapel was also in great need of repair, especially the ceiling.

Without intervention and dedicated workmanship, the chapel would deteriorate even more. This remarkable edifice has remained for centuries but unfortunately, most young people, being preoccupied with their electronic gadgets are oblivious to the beauty of churches and chapels. They have no desire to cherish or preserve such

history. That was evident to me at the Saint Solange mass at the church. There were no more than a handful of young people at the service. The majority of the attendees were all aged. Even the priest. It would pain me deeply to get this far and walk away without trying to do all I could do to restore the chapel to its former simple beauty.

As we walked out of the chapel, Thierry was closing the door and securing his precious key back into his pocket, Jocelyn turned to me and asked, "Would you like to see where she was killed? It's not far from here, we can actually walk." "Of course, I would love to go." By now, Josiane who does not believe or practice any religious faith, was more than ready to leave. I, on the other hand, would not allow that to stop me from experiencing another milestone of my pilgrimage.

During my exhilarating tour of the chapel, Josiane sat under a tree reading her book. Jacques on the other hand, came along and seemed to have been touched by my infatuation and belief in Saint Solange. So Jocelyn, Thierry, Jacques and I started on our next adventure, walking the phenomenal, faith-filled path that Solange took from the river where she was decapitated to the church. Jocelyn was leading the group. From the door of the chapel, she turned left, then proceeded to walk a straight path behind the chapel. We then came face to face with a very tall wooden cross that is also associated with Saint Solange. The wooden cross was riddled with chop marks and heavy scratches. This was due to its antiquity and also its history. Jocelyn explained that visitors come with knives and pull out small pieces of the cross to take home or to their business, for blessings or good luck. Others

will take pieces of the wood to carry on their body for healing or protection. Obviously, it's all about ones' belief. The importance of these activities however, is the outcome. If one is sick and believes that by carrying in one's pocket, a chip of the cross from Saint Solange Chapel will improve their health and the person is cured, who can judge this persons faith?

Jocelyn and I were walking faster than Thierry and Jacques. I felt as though we were walking to infinity. In front of us was open space. On both sides of us was land and in the distance were tall trees. We walked and walked on the dirt and gravel path. From a distance I could vaguely see what resembled the headless statue that I saw on the internet. I started to walk faster and faster,

eventually leaving Jocelyn at some distance behind me, Thierry and Jacques were even farther away.

As the statue became clearer, I could even hear the noise of the river rippling along the bank, and the swishing of the tall trees. I was by now within a few feet of the statue. In front of me, almost at a touching distance was an old, cement colored monument of a headless female body erected just at the beginning of the river.

The statue, incredible as it was to see for the first time, was not the only surprise. What followed at that moment was actually heart pounding. Suddenly out of the bushes, in between the trees, a tall man popped out and stood a few feet in front of me! He seemed to have appeared out of nowhere. I am sure my heart skipped a few beats from the shock of the encounter with this stranger. It was

obvious to him as well that I was startled by his unexpected presence. Fortunately I was not alone for too much longer. Jocelyn was only a few steps behind me and Thierry and Jacques eventually joined us. Even so, during that split-second encounter, I felt the presence of danger. It flashed through my mind that my life so closely paralleled the Saint, I was afraid I would meet the same fate right at that spot where she tragically died. With those scary thoughts bombarding my mind, I admit that if I had ventured alone on this deserted road and encountered this strange man, I think I would have died of a heart attack.

When Jocelyn arrived on the scene minutes later, my heart was still racing uncontrollably. From the look on her face, it was obvious that she was just as surprised to see this man as I was. With my

friends at my side, my fear began to fade. When I took a better look and focused as he came closer, I could see that he looked like a perfect gentleman. He was dressed in a brown blazer, a white shirt, a very nice burgundy tie and beige trousers. He was well groomed and very distinguished with a black mustache and a grey beard. Nevertheless his presence was a distraction, temporarily robbing me of the excitement of my long awaited discovery. Here I was in great anticipation of a genuine spiritual encounter and fear walked in threatening to overshadow what I had hoped to experience by walking in the footsteps of Saint Solange. Soon all five of us moved past the fears and distractions. We began talking and sharing stories. The gentleman from the bushes showed us that he had brought along a Bible that was on a folding table near his car. It was concealed by the bushes.

Saint Solange Admirer and I

He told us that he too, was an admirer of Saint Solange and that his birthday was also on May 10th, the same day of Saint Solanges' death. So he and I shared the same date of birth. It seemed to me that as Solange died, a new Solanges was born to continue her mission even if it took me centuries to get here. The stranger told us, that he comes to the river where Solange was killed every year, to spend time in prayer with Saint Solange as his personal birthday celebration. I was overwhelmed with everything I was experiencing. Meeting this stranger at the river where Saint Solange was martyred. Sharing the same date of birth…how likely is that? Indeed, what are the chances that something like that would happen? All of these disjointed fragments were fusing in my mind as major pieces to an extraordinary story. The more he talked, the more astonished we became. Gone was the notion of fear. So at his behest, we followed him closer to his car. He picked up his prayer book from the little table and read a prayer to Saint Solange, similar to the prayer that was recited during mass earlier during the day, at the celebration at the church.

The prayer read at the church earlier that day was:

"On this anniversary day, Saint Solange, patron of Berry, we come here to implore you as our ancestors did after they had mistreated you in this locality. We remember the devotions you spread on Berry, witness of your birth on this earthly life and in heaven. We ask you to present our intentions to God, our father. May, by your intercession, humility live in peace and unity. May the youth, like you, submit their life to God. May

this place see, until the end of time, pilgrims coming to pray for themselves, their families, their friends and the entire church. Finally, at the end of our pilgrimage on earth, we enter like you, in the glory of God . Amen."

This experience was enough to take my breath away. I was already reeling from the high expectation of my experience of treading on the very path of Saint Solange. I wanted to linger in the moment, drawing in all my thoughts of her journey as she walked, decapitated. I never expected to experience such an encounter with a stranger near the river where she was struck down. At first it was startling, but it grew in significance. It boldly served to reinforce in my mind, the spirituality of the journey I was undertaking. Neither of us, the stranger nor I, would have any

way of ever meeting if it had not been for Saint Solange. It was as if she had summoned both of us there at the same time. I suspect the gentleman's faith was strengthened to see that another soul cared as much as he did about the saint, to travel so far, in order to be in her presence. For me, it gave me a first-hand understanding of how the humility and holiness of Saint Solange still lives in the hearts and minds of others. For both of us, I dare say, the experience was unforgettable and fulfilling in the knowledge that no one could have arranged such a divine encounter but God.

From my first experience in the village, one major take-away for me was how the people were so nice to me. I was a perfect stranger - and yes... a black woman. They gave me prayer books, images and medallions of Saint Solange. Jocelyn and her

husband invited me to return to Saint Solange for Tuesday, the nineteenth of May... to stay with them, because she wanted me to participate in a novena for Saint Solange. The novena is nine days of prayer, ending in a celebration on Pentecostal Monday. I accepted and promised to return.

We left Saint Solange village, took some more pictures and headed back to the home of my cousin Josiane and her husband Jacques, in Gif-Sur - Yvette...a drive of two and a half hours, back to this province outside Paris. I spent the next three weeks at their home, waiting for Pentecostal Sunday, to return to Saint Solange village for the big celebration.

As much as I wanted to return to the village and spend the nine novena days in prayer with my newly-found friend Jocelyn, my cousin Josiane felt strongly that I should not return to Bourges alone and live with the couple we had just recently met. So far we had only spent a few hours together at lunch getting acquainted with eachother. I decided to listen to my cousin. I stayed at Josiane's home for those three weeks, but developed an almost constant communication with Jocelyn.

On Saturday morning, the 23rd of May, Jacques, Josiane and I drove to Paris to collect Clifford from the airport. He made the trip to accompany me back to Bourges for the Pentecostal Monday procession, since Jacques had to work and would not be able to drive me back to Bourges. Luckily, his flight was on time and there was no drama with his luggage. We drove to Gif-Sur-Yvette, spent some time at their house, went to lunch at a

great Chinese restaurant, said our goodbyes and drove off to Saint Solange village in Jacques' car.

As I reflected on all that had occurred, I felt that I was experiencing bits of heaven, here on earth. I felt as if I were walking on clouds, which may be the best way to describe the excitement I felt. I knew this feeling would only become more intense as I approached Saint Solange village. We arrived in the village at five-thirty in the evening. As we made the left turn off the main road into the village, there was a big sign at the side of the road that read: Ste SOLANGE. We stopped the car and took pictures at the sign. For Clifford and I, the sign cemented the notion in our minds, that we were actually in the village about which we had spoken so often. Reality was sinking in, which was electrifying. This was really "it," and there was still more to see and know. We continued down a long, winding dirt road, stopping at a little cottage called the "Mezier Residence." It was a bed and

Ste Solange Village Road Sign

breakfast that Jocelyn had arranged for us to stay for the weekend, since there are no hotels in

the village. Clifford and I dropped our bags, and my new friend Jocelyn, who had met us at the cottage so quickly, spirited us away to the birthplace of Saint Solange and her town. According to the most recent statistics, the population of Saint Solange was about twelve hundred, with four hundred fifty-six main residences, eighteen occasional or secondary homes and twenty-seven vacant ones. As we toured the village, we felt that we were stepping back into antiquity. The village's spartan cleanliness, however, gave it a fresh look, as if it awaited something or someone that would bring a breath of new life. Maybe it waited for an interested tourist like me, who has a healthy respect for history and a keen eye for future preservation. As we toured the birthplace, a rugged, old cross attracted our interest. The home in which Saint Solange was reared had been razed centuries ago, but the cross marked the site where she was born. On the pedestal which supported it, there was no date. I wondered how the cross figured in her life.

Solanges and Jocelyn at the birthplace of Saint Solange

Did the family gather there to pray? Is this where she was when she dedicated her life to Christ? Was this the spot where she spent time kneeling in prayer? Whatever truth that could be gleaned, I

could only imagine the tenacity of this symbol of her faith that remained unmovable and unshakeable for twelve centuries. Clifford and I could have remained at the site for hours, reflecting on the significance of the cross, but we had to move on. We stopped at Jocelyn's for a drink, found a nice restaurant in town for dinner and ended this long, historic day back at the bed and breakfast... tired but too excited for much sleep.

Sunday morning came quickly, bringing with it such excitement that my entire mind and body felt like they were being flooded with bubbles of pure delight. It was Sunday, but my mind kept flashing forward to Monday, because on that day I would be in the procession of this saint, whose spirit (I believe) has touched mine. It is almost like waking up from a dream, to wonder if it were really

happening. At this moment, my mind returned to Sunday morning, because it was time for our continental breakfast, before heading off to church. Because Saint Solange village has two churches, the mass alternates between the two, thus assuring a larger congregation at the only available Sunday service. Fortunately for me, I was able to attend mass at each of the two, on two separate Sunday visits. After mass we had some light refreshments at Jocelyn's house. Then, Clifford and I headed back to Bourges, where the activities were. We had a great lunch at the Auberge Provincial, toured the Cathedral of Bourges and walked La Marais...a very long route of beautiful gardens and rivers. When we finally returned to the cottage, we were very tired and ready for bed. Finally, the long-awaited event - Pentecostal Monday - was actually upon us. I had conceived of

it as my divine assignment. It was one of the two main events that had the spiritual power to lift me from my comfortable home in Washington, DC, and had caused me to travel to Bourges - a place of which, until recently, I had never known.

Pentecostal Monday was my date with destiny, although there was one more incident that further cemented my connection with Saint Solange. On Saturday, "out of the blue," as Jocelyn and I were exploring the village, Jocelyn abruptly stopped and turned toward me. She looked me straight in the eye, grabbed my arms and frantically said, "Oh my God! I forgot to tell you that Saint Saint Solange's colors are red and white, which we will wear in the procession."

Seeing how deeply ashamed she was by this apparent omission, I felt tears well up in my eyes. I

knew she understood the significance of this occasion to me. What she did not know, however, was that I had purchased a brand new white dress, and had carried with me red jewelry, specifically to wear on Pentecostal Monday, during the procession. Who knew that Saint Solange's colors were red and white? I certainly did not. Now I was certain that this journey was filled, not with mere coincidences, but with God's mysterious hand in my life. There is no other way to explain how, of all the possible combinations of wardrobe colors I might have chosen, I had purchased and chosen the exact colors favored by Saint Solange. When you see pictures of the procession, you will see me in my brand new white dress, wearing red jewelry and looking fabulous... for Saint Solange.

Solanges in White and Red for the

Saint Solange Pentecostal Monday Procession

On the morning of the service, we arrived a bit early. It was about nine thirty and the procession would not begin until eleven o' clock. I

was amazed at the amount of people who were already gathered at the church, along with others in their cars. We made our way into the church, where another shock awaited me; the replica of Saint Solange that had been in a glass case at the chapel, was on display. People were bringing her flowers and depositing them all around her and on the replica itself. Others were touching her and praying over her. If I had only known, I might have claimed a front row seat... I could have brought her flowers! I made a mental note to myself, that this opportunity would warrant a return visit to the village on Pentecostal Monday.

Saint Solange Replica adorned for

Pentecostal Monday mass

As the procession began, every statue and every tapestry of Saint Solange was taken down from the walls and the ceiling of the church and chapel, to be carried during the procession. There were about ten priests, including the Archbishop of Bourges, in the vestibule of the church, ready to celebrate mass – so I thought.

To my astonishment however, mass did not precede the procession. Instead, four women who were seated next to the replica of Saint Solange, got up. Others assisted in placing the full-sized replica on their shoulders. After a short prayer service, all the statues were now placed on the shoulders of select people. Then, everyone, including the priests, assembled in specific order. There were small children, boys and girls, dressed in Saint Solange's red and white village costumes. There was also a group of Portuguese worshippers, dressed in their native costumes. They were so beautiful. I am told the Portuguese have adopted Saint Solange. They supported and contributed to the renovation of the chapel in past years and they come in large groups every year for Pentecostal Monday.

Saint Solange Pentecostal Monday Procession

Gathering of Priests

As we processed from the church to the chapel, the crowd stopped at three stations for prayer and singing. It was very moving, somewhat like the Stations of the Cross in the Via Dolorosa of Jerusalem, where Jesus is depicted carrying His cross on the way to the Crucifixion. I was fortunate to be able to note the similarity; I had walked the

Via Dolorosa in Jerusalem on an earlier pilgrimage. I relived that day as I participated in this procession for Saint Solange. As we walked, the church choir rode in a van, singing sacred hymns through speakers that could be heard throughout the processional. It was a solemn occasion that tugged at my mind, body and spirit.

My heart overflowed with joy. After walking for about half a mile, the procession ended, in front of the Saint Solange chapel. Because her chapel is very small, a temporary elevated altar was built outside, in front of the chapel, where an outdoor service could be held. There were lots of benches for the participants, and on each side of the altar was a covered section for the choir and a special place for the children who would participate in the

Saint Solange Pentecostal Monday Procession

service. There were lots of cars parked on both sides of the long, unpaved road to the chapel, as well as multiple tables for the vendors who sold all kinds of artifacts related to Saint Solange.

Saint Solanges Chapel outdoor service

The weather pleasantly affirmed the outdoor procession. It was neither too hot, nor too cold, but partly cloudy with a subtle chill in the air. Just a

sweater sufficed for the brisk walk of the procession. Shortly after the celebrant began the mass with the opening prayer, the weather made a rather surprising major shift... "out of the blue." The sun appeared between the trees and beamed brightly for about ten minutes, with a ray illuminating the fabric on the altar. The quick change in the atmosphere captured my attention. I remember being happy to see the sun, but as quickly as it appeared, the sun then disappeared. At first, the shift did not seem so unusual, because it is not abnormal for the sun to make an appearance for a few minutes (or hours), then go into hiding. Once again, mass continued, but just as the priest began to pray over the bread and wine in preparation for communion, a fine mist of rain began to fall on the congregation, similar to the mist one feels when the priest blesses palms during

Palm Sunday services. The only difference here was that the mist came from the sky and stopped as suddenly as it had started.

To many congregants around me, the atmospheric transitions were another example of supernatural manifestations. They saw this as an act of God - a visitation where every year Saint Solange makes herself known to the congregation through this ceremony. It went from cloudy to sunny, to misty rain, all in a matter of minutes. How unusual! It is my nature to be skeptical, but this experience has provided me with enough spiritual evidence that I had no trouble believing what most villagers believe... that Saint Solange was present at the mass, and that she wanted the congregation to know that she was their protector. Surely this was supernatural. It is not something that one can fully

understand except through faith, and by being there to experience it first-hand.

I was there and no one can convince me that the elements did not change in a very extraordinary way. I saw the clouds and the sun and I felt the mist on our faces, like a baptismal blessing. After the service there was an aura of godliness that permeated the atmosphere as everyone was talking about the celestial changes occurring at the appropriate time during the mass. The rest of the day was cloudy again. There was no more sun and no more mist. It was as if Saint Solange did what she had done for centuries - making a spiritual appearance to strengthen believers in their faith in Jesus Christ. Her appearance compelled us to examine our lives in comparison to her walk with Jesus Christ. Solange as a young girl was so firmly committed to Jesus that she surrendered her life rather than rescind her vow of purity. How committed are we to Jesus? How much of our lives do we surrender to Him? Surely our walk of faith should be quickened by her example.

In contrast, none of us are called to such extreme acts of faith. Some well-meaning Christians think even providing for the sick or encouraging the broken-hearted is too much to do. Being here and thinking how love drove Jesus to die for our sins, and thinking how Saint Solange's love drove her to surrender her life to Him makes me wonder: shouldn't we be more committed Christians, in light of these examples of love in action?

As promised, Jocelyn and her husband tried to get me to carry the life-sized replica of Saint Solange during the procession, but I was not able to do so. A mother had requested that only her four daughters should carry the replica for the entire length of the procession. This wish was granted to her before I even knew about Saint Solange.

Jocelyn, however, had given me another assignment during the mass in front of the chapel. I was asked to be one of the people who walked through the crowd with a basket to accept the offerings during the mass. I eagerly accepted this assignment. In doing so, however, I saw a larger message. I saw how badly the chapel was in need of restoration, and I felt a deep desire and commitment to this project. Because of this, I will be contributing to it and helping to raise funds, by creating opportunities such as this book you now hold, to bring awareness of this saint to the rest of the world, as I believe should be done.

Rendering of future Saint Solange Chapel

Once the ceremonies were over, Clifford and I went to clear out our little cottage, then stopped at Jocelyn's for lunch and said our farewells.

The goodbye between Jocelyn and I became very emotional. She called me her American sister, to whom she had been introduced by Saint Solange. I was so blessed that she approached me after mass and became my guardian angel. I believe God was acting anonymously when He assigned Jocelyn to take care of me during my pilgrimage... guiding and protecting me along the way.

In a final reflection, I must share that I started this adventure totally blind, not knowing what to expect. I came out of it with a deeper level of spirituality and walking closer with God. I would encourage everyone to follow his or her intuition. To be courageous and not to allow the unknown to keep him or her from following that dream. Never put off until tomorrow what you can do today, because tomorrow may never come. I am happy

that I made this trip. I have grown spiritually. I hope that after reading my adventurous story, you too will have gained a deeper level of awareness of your own personal faith. Know your purpose in life and combine that purpose with your faith and follow your heart. This formula will lead you to peace and success, as you become a truly great human being in the eyes of God.

A note from Solanges

You may wonder why there is an "s" at the end of my name. Well, it was not my parents' decision. I thought it would be cute, distinctive and different to add an "s" at the end of my name: I did it many years ago when I was preparing my passport to travel abroad. So now you have it. I am (perhaps) the only Solanges in the world that you will ever meet that has an "s" at the end of her name. I hope you enjoyed reading this book as much as I enjoyed sharing the story with you.

~Solanges Vivens

About the Author

Solanges Vivens migrated to the United States from Haiti in search of a better life. She began her journey in New York City as a French-speaking teenager who had to learn the English language. After working in a series of factories for minimum wage and working in the infant nursery of a hospital as a Nursing Assistant, she then spent three transforming years of her life as an au pair for three children in the home of a wealthy white family. In that setting, aided by the strong Christian roots of her family, she fit together the pieces of her own success and learned to put her faith into action, seeking opportunities to offer help, hope and healing to those in need, a practice which remains a guiding light in her life today. As a young Haitian-American adult, it became clear to her that

only through education and hard work could she improve her socio-economic situation. As she mastered the English language she also developed an educational strategy and enrolled in nursing school and became a Licensed Practical Nurse. Then, with further education, she progressed to become a Registered Nurse. Solanges is never satisfied. After becoming a Registered Nurse, she continued her quest by earning a Bachelors' degree in Nursing from Long Island University, followed by a Masters' degree in Health Services Administration from Georgetown University and finally, a Doctoral degree in Humane Letters from Voorhees College. Manifesting the business savvy of her father, Solanges worked hard to become a Nursing Supervisor and then a Director of Nursing, before becoming a Nursing Home Administrator and finally a Nursing Home and Healthcare Entrepreneur.

A resident of the District of Columbia, she is known for spending many sleepless nights, planning and preparing creative and effective strategies for improving her life and the lives of others. She is a mother and a grandmother, and for the past thirty-nine years she has made a passion of caring for seniors and the disabled. She has published a great many articles on topics in the field of Nursing and Healthcare.

Solanges is also a woman of commitment. She expresses that commitment with her time, talents and treasures. This book is a testament to Solanges' commitment of time and talent in pursuing her spiritual calling. By travel through books and by actual travel, on planes and in cars to chapels abroad, Solanges has made an apparent

historical discovery which (in turn) became a personal discovery and a mirror into herself.

Solanges' commitment of time and talent has also blossomed into a commitment of her treasures. Along with publishing this book, she is launching a global drive to raise funds for the Saint Solange chapel in Bourges, France, where believers gather yearly to partake in ceremonies on Pentecostal Monday, in honor of this venerable saint.

RESEARCH AND RESOURCE MATERIALS

FOR SAINT SOLANGE

Badin and Quentin: Géographie départmentale, classique et administrative de la France, département du Cher, Paris, 1847

Bull, Marcus Graham and Catherine Léglu, The world of Eleanor of Aquitane : literature and society in southern France, The Boydell Press, 2005

CATHOLIC ONLINE: Saints and angels

The Catholic Encyclopedia: An International Work of Reference on the Constitution, Doctrine, Discipline and History of the Catholic Church, also referred to as the Old Catholic Encyclopedia and the Original Catholic Encyclopedia.

Defrasne, Jean: Mystères et légendes du Berry Cabedita, Yens –sur-Morges (Switzerland), 2006

Dolouc, Jean : Sainte Solange du paganisme au christianisme published on the site Thibault Isabel, http://www.thibaultisabel.com/page54.html

http://faithofthefatherssaints.blogspot.com/2005/09

FaithND on website of the University of Notre Dame Alumni

Guerin, Paul: Les petits Bollandistes : Vie des saintes, Volume 5, 7th edition, Paris, 1876

The Little Bollandists: Lives of the Saints, Volume 5

E.W. Kemp: Alexander III and the Canonization of Saints,

Transactions of the Royal Historical Society 4th Series, Volume 27 (1945) 14-16

Lapaire, Hugues: "Saint Solange", Les légendes berrichonnes : legendes rustiques, historiques et religeuses,

Superstitions du Haut & Bas-Berry Champrond-en-Gâtine, Editions du Colombier, 2003

Raynal Louis : Histoire du Berry depuis les temps les plus anciens jusqu'en 1789 Vermeil, 1844-1847, p.313 ff

William H. Woestman, O.M.I, ed, Canonization : Theology, History, Process (Ottawa, Canada: Saint Paul University, 2002), 28

Antoine Chevalier: Manual du Pelerin de Sainte Solange

Marie Legeret : Sainte Solange Patrone du Berry Hier et aujoud'hui-Les lieu Saints.